Fancy Mice
KW-224

CONTENTS

Photo credits: Dr. Herbert R. Axelrod, H. Bielfeld, Michael Gilroy, and E. Jukes.

Opposite: Dove and Champagne Tan mice.

1995 Edition

Distributed in the UNITED STATES to the Pet Trade by T.F.H. Publications, Inc., One T.F.H. Plaza, Neptune City, NJ 07753; distributed in the UNITED STATES to the Bookstore and Library Trade by National Book Network, Inc. 4720 Boston Way, Lanham MD 20706; in CANADA to the Pet Trade by H & L Pet Supplies Inc., 27 Kingston Crescent, Kitchener, Ontario N2B 2T6; Rolf C. Hagen Ltd., 3225 Sartelon Street, Montreal 382 Quebec; in CANADA to the Book Trade by Vanwell Publishing Ltd., 1 Northrup Crescent, St. Catharines, Ontario L2M 6P5 ; in ENGLAND by T.F.H. Publications, PO Box 15, Waterlooville PO7 6BQ; in AUSTRALIA AND THE SOUTH PACIFIC by T.F.H. (Australia), Pty. Ltd., Box 149, Brookvale 2100 N.S.W., Australia; in NEW ZEALAND by Brooklands Aquarium Ltd. 5 McGiven Drive, New Plymouth, RD1 New Zealand; in Japan by T.F.H. Publications, Japan—Jiro Tsuda, 10-12-3 Ohjidai, Sakura, Chiba 285, Japan; in SOUTH AFRICA by Lopis (Pty) Ltd., P.O. Box 39127, Booysens, 2016, Johannesburg, South Africa. Published by T.F.H. Publications, Inc.
MANUFACTURED IN THE UNITED STATES OF AMERICA
BY T.F.H. PUBLICATIONS, INC.

FANCY MICE

CHRIS HENWOOD

INTRODUCTION

To a great many youngsters a pet mouse is their first introduction to the pleasures, and more importantly, the responsibilities, of caring for a living, furry creature. It is often these young owners' interest in

Mice are enjoyable and amusing pets that have continued to grow in popularity throughout the years.

the mouse that encourages them to go on keeping other pets at a later period in their lives. But equally, some young mouse owners retain their first love and begin a lifelong devotion to the breeding and exhibiting of fancy mice—a hobby that worldwide absorbs the time of thousands of devoted people of both sexes and of all ages.

The domesticated or fancy mouse has been put to many different uses over the centuries. As an example, the Greeks of ancient times used them as a means of telling the future. The medical profession has used them in research to cure any number of ills, from diabetes to warts to cancer. Mice have been used to test the air quality in mines and in early submarines and have even been shot into space.

Above all, the mouse is the

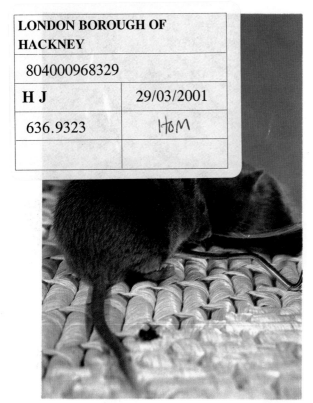

creature that has been most extensively used in medical, scientific, and genetic research. In fact today if you describe the domesticated house or fancy mouse as existing in a number of colors, you are making an understatement, to say the least. They can be black or white, yellow, blue or red, smooth, curly and longhaired or a combination of any one of these. In fact there are about 700 different color and coat varieties. In actual terms however, you can only expect really to be able to see or find about 50 or so of these at any one time.

The fancy mouse is, of course, the domesticated form of the wild house mouse. The house mouse has spread all over the world from its original home in the central and southern parts of Asia. There are a number of different

subspecies with slightly different habits. This enables the house mouse to colonize almost any habitat where food and shelter are provided by man. As a result, the species is very widespread, inhabiting

There are literally hundreds and hundreds of color varieties of mice, but many of them are not easily available.

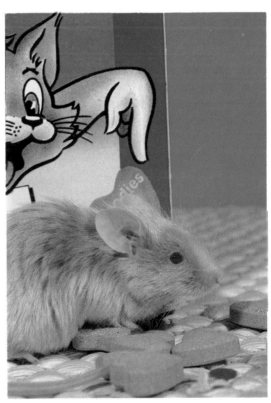

Introduction

all areas of the world and causing widespread damage in many areas.

IS A MOUSE RIGHT FOR YOU?

Every pet, however small, will change the life of its owner and the other members of the household. If you are thinking of obtaining a mouse or mice, then it is important that all the family members should discuss whether or not they wish to share their home with these creatures.

It is certainly not very difficult to take care of a mouse or several mice, but keep in mind that mice are prolific breeders, and you can easily end up caring for *many* mice. It is a good idea to consider what you are letting yourself in for. Ask the following questions:

1. Does every member of the family agree to your obtaining a mouse or mice?

2. Does everyone like mice?

3. Will other members of the family look after your mice when you are unable to?

4. Are you prepared to buy a suitable cage for your animal(s) of the correct size, complete with the best accessories?

5. Do you have at least an hour per day that you are prepared to give up to play with your mice and to take care of them?

6. Can you cope with a sick mouse and the fact that mice are not long-lived animals?

If you can say "yes" to all these, I am sure that you will make a very good owner. However, if you can't then I would suggest that you think again about obtaining a mouse as a pet.

Opposite: *Mice are inquisitive little characters that will delight you with their antics.*

HOUSING

Almost every person you will speak to about mice will have their own ideas as to the correct way in which to keep them and I suppose that I am no exception. Some of my ideas are very different from those of some of my friends. All I can say is that what I write here and, for that matter throughout this book, are what has worked and does work for me (tried and tested).

The first thing to remember is that your pet's cage will become the individual animal's territory; its home base. This it will scentmark and defend against intrusion by members of its own species and even you at times. It should also not be disturbed too often by too much cleaning out.

The location or siting of the

A hand-tame mouse of the satin variety. It is best to have your new mouse's housing prepared before you bring him home. Opposite: *An assortment of mice exhibiting several color varieties.*

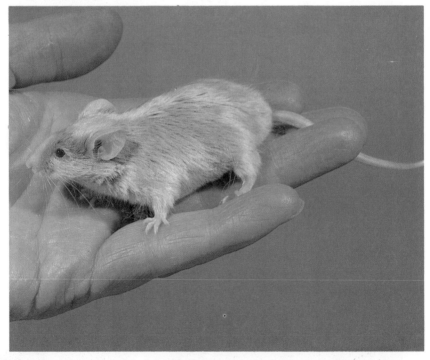

cage is as important as the cage itself. Its location should be neither too hot nor too cold, too humid nor too dry. But having said all this, it is important to remember the real function of a cage is the very obvious one: to confine the inhabitants and to isolate them into the required units, i.e., small groups, pairs or individuals.

There are many different kinds of rodent or mouse cages available commercially. Which of these you eventually decide to use will undoubtedly depend on the numbers of animals kept and where the cage will be sited. However, whichever cage(s) is chosen, they should all meet the following requirements:

1. They must be escape-proof. Tops must close securely and easily without hurting either the mouse or its owner.

2. The metal parts, if any, should in no way be able to hurt either the animals or the humans handling the cage.

3. It should be easy to remove and replace animals.

4. There must be sufficient space for necessary food and water to last for at least 48 hours.

5. The cage must be easy to clean.

6. It must have adequate ventilation.

7. It should have a much longer life span than that of a single mouse.

Commercial cages come in a wide variety of sizes, shapes and construction, from simple homes for a single animal to vast complexes capable of containing large colonies. Housing purchased at your local pet shop is easy to use, economical, and readily available. You may even find kits that include all the preliminary materials necessary for starting this hobby.

Choose a cage as large as possible, at least two feet square, with a depth that enables the mouse to stand on its hindlegs and only just be able to touch the roof. A ten-gallon all-glass aquarium is

Opposite: One of the functions of a mouse's tail is to help the animal maintain its balance.

ideal. If an aquarium is used, you will need to provide a fitted wire top. Remember, mice can squeeze through quite small holes so the mesh must be of a suitable size, no more than $1/4$ inch square.

Mice, particularly adult males, can be very smelly; therefore a mouse's home needs to be easily cleaned. It is advisable, if the cage is to be kept in the house rather than in a shed, to avoid cages made of wood. Although wooden cages may be cheaper than others, they are not always practical. The wood will soak up urine and will remain damp. Cages made of plastic, glass or stainless steel are all highly recommended. A plastic or metal cage is easily cleaned; it is also light enough to be transported and requires very little maintenance to keep it in good condition. You can also say the same for glass aquaria, but these do tend to be heavier.

Food should be supplied in bowls, which are often an integral part of the cage. Don't forget that any cover of an aquarium should provide adequate ventilation. All cages should have a simple but strong latch that is easy to lock but difficult for your pet to open.

A pet shop will have various toys to provide your pet with amusement. Never use childrens' toys because mice chew off the plastic and swallow it. By far, the best toy is the exercise wheel. It is a great accessory that mice really love. With mice, it really doesn't matter whether the wheel is of the solid type or a spoked one.

Whatever type of cage you eventually decide upon, place plenty of litter or bedding in the cage to allow your mouse to move it around and create the desired terrain. A two- to three-inch layer of bedding is best. Bedding materials can be of various different types, but I prefer wood shavings. Spread lots of shavings over the bottom of the cage so that the mouse can move it around to suit its needs: don't pile it up in one corner of the cage. Some mice will hide food in certain areas of the cage, usually well away from the nest area. Mice rearrange the bedding quite often. This behavior creates another cage consideration. Some metal cages are constructed with a wire top and sides, with only an inch or two of closed barriers along the bottom edges of the sides. As the bedding is moved about the cage, quite a lot of it is scattered about the outside of it. Therefore, if a cage of this type is considered, to my mind it should have a solid back and sides, with a barrier along the front of at least three to four inches in height. Some cages come with removable clear plastic or glass barriers along the cage front. This allows you to see your mouse but keeps the bedding in the cage. The floor litter needs to be removed entirely at weekly intervals and replaced with a fresh supply. Don't clean too often, especially the quarters of male mice, as this only makes them

A mouse and his "cousin": a gerbil. Both of these animals are rodents.

scentmark their cages even more. Thorough cage cleaning is an essential part of your regular routine, or at least it should become so. Every few weeks, wash the cage with hot, soapy water and a stiff brush. Of course when a female has a litter of babies, you should not clean out the cage as this will upset the mother and she may even kill her litter.

Nests can be made of many different materials, but by far the best are paper bedding and/or hay. Hay, not straw, is particularly good as mice do rather like to eat some of the hay and it cleans their coats as they push their way through it. Always avoid the cotton wool type bedding, as this can lead to problems if eaten by your mouse. Some commercial cages provide special nest box areas for mice, and these are very useful as it prevents the babies and bedding from being scattered around the cage, either by the mother or by wandering away by themselves.

Perhaps the major advantage of using an aquarium over using a commercial cage is that with an aquarium, you can provide your mouse with a much deeper litter base and thus more area to move around and also more areas on which to climb and jump about. Remember that mice really do enjoy climbing about and thus anything that you can provide for them to climb about on will be appreciated. Branches cut from fruit trees, such as apple or pear, are very useful as they provide a number of different diameters to exercise the feet and claws. (Be sure the branches have not been chemically treated.)

HOUSING FOR FANCY MICE

The housing of the show fancy mouse in numbers really differs from the housing of a single or small group of pet mice. If you intend to breed mice for showing or for colors, then it is unlikely that you will be able to keep the number required in the house. The

Opposite, top: *Pet shops stock a variety of housing units that are suitable for mice and that come equipped with all of the necessary cage accessories. Whatever kind of housing you choose, be sure that it is durable and easy to maintain.* **Opposite, bottom:** *Provide your mouse with high-absorbency bedding and change it on a regular basis to prevent the buildup of harmful bacteria. Photos courtesy Rolf C. Hagen Corp.*

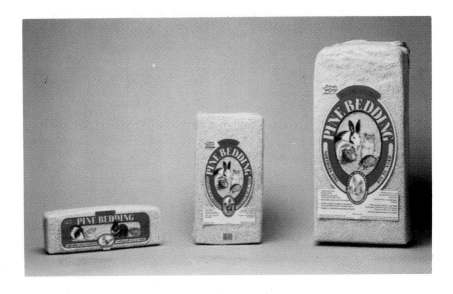

majority of show breeders accommodate their stock in an outhouse—either a wooden or brick shed—situated in the garden. Most fanciers have a shed in the region of 8' x 5' or 10' x 6'. A shed of this size will easily house several hundred mice if necessary and still leave you quite a lot of space.

It is essential that any shed, be it brick or wooden, be dry and draft-proof. A large shed is better than a small one simply because it allows you to expand, although many successful studs have been kept in quite tiny areas. However, do not be tempted to have too large a shed as this will be subject to sudden temperature changes. A wooden shed should be raised at least 12 inches off the ground. This prevents excess dampness in the shed and allows fresh air to circulate. Good ventilation for the occupants is most important. I would suggest that at least one window should be made to open. Mice are very hardy, so the window can be left open at all times except in extreme cold weather or when there is snow or fog. In the summer, it is a good idea to provide an all-wire door over the gap left

when the normal door is left open. This wire door will prevent the entry of cats, rats, wild mice or other predators. It is important to also permanently wire over the open window for the very same reasons.

Additionally, it is a good idea to insulate the wall and roof of the shed. This may be carried out in a number of different ways. Probably the easiest is fiber glass covered with a facing of decorative hard board. Some fanciers use heating of one form or another; others do not. It depends on the size of the shed and the number of its occupants. However, the mice themselves, if healthy and well managed, should survive even the hardest winter without heating, although it should be borne in mind that if this is the case they do not breed quite so regularly. Electric light is, to

Opposite: *Your pet should have the opportunity for regular exercise. Pet shops stock a full line of mouse amusement devices, in addition to basic items such as food and bedding.*

my mind, a necessity and in hot weather an electric fan would be helpful.

Actually planning the layout of the shed or mousery must reflect individual tastes. To be honest, there are no hard and fast rules to follow. A good solid table top is very useful. It is best situated beneath the window so that you can inspect stock in natural light. The table top can serve as a storage area for sawdust, hay, and food, the latter preferably in a mouse-proof tin. Along the back of the shed can be stacked mouse boxes—either on top of each other or on shelves or special racks.

Although due to the smell it is not advisable to keep mice in wooden cages in the house, this is not quite as true in your mousery. Smells out here, being much better ventilated, are not so offensive.

Since I am not a good carpenter, although I do try, I find it easier to buy breeding box cages in the form of secondhand laboratory cages. These are quite expensive but have the advantage of a long life and may be used for many different species of rodent—not just fancy mice. However, over the years the majority of

owners of fancy mice, with whom I am acquainted, have retained their breeding stocks in wooden breeding boxes. These are quite easy to make even for someone as bad at carpentry as I.

If you do attempt to make your own cages, try to avoid using soft woods. These absorb moisture more easily and are also much easier for the mice to chew through. I would suggest that the best wood to use would be one of the hardwood plywoods. If you can manage to obtain a large sheet of 2.5m x 1.25m (in the United States the standard size would be 4 feet by 8 feet) you should be able to make 8 or even 9 cages out of it. You should work out the exact measurements of the sides, ends, bottom and top of your boxes perhaps by drawing them on paper before transferring them to the plywood sheet. In this way you will keep wastage to a minimum. A suitably sized box for breeding is: 16 3/8" (long) x 7 3/4" (wide) x 6 1/4" (high) or 40cms x 20cms x 15cms. So for a box this size you need two sides 16 3/8" x 6 1/4" (A&B), one bottom 16 x 6 7/8" (C), one lid 15 5/8" x 6 7/8" (D), one back 6

⁷/₈" x 5 ⁷/₈" (E), and two pieces of 6 ⁷/₈" x 2 ¹/₂" (F) and 6 ⁷/₈" x 1 ¹/₄" (G) for the front.

The pieces may be fitted together in the following order:

1. Fix the back (E) to the base (C).

2. Add the bottom front (F).

3. Check that the joints are square; then add one side (A).

4. Add second side (B).

5. Add second front section (G) ensuring it is level with the top of the sides.

6. Finally, turn the box on its end and using wire staples, attach wire mesh or zinc over the gap you have left between the two front sections.

7. The lid. This should be the exact size of the top; it must fit tightly or the edges will be chewed by the mice. Around the edges battens should be attached so that it does not fall into the box.

The entire box may be varnished so that it will last longer.

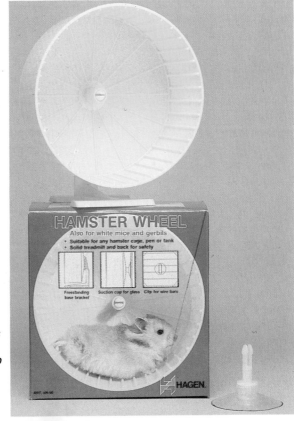

You can choose from a variety of toys and gadgets that will amuse your pet and help to keep it active. Photo courtesy Rolf C. Hagen Corp.

FEEDING

Diets for mice vary in the wild almost as much as the areas from which they come. Mice are known to inhabit deep freezers storing meat, on which they feed. Ancient tombs, unpopulated islands, even candle stores, have found their stocks eaten by mice. Mice tend to eat what they can find. However, this is not to say that these items are good for them.

In captivity you, the owner, have the ability to provide your pets with exactly the correct diet required by them so they remain fit and healthy. As with a lot of points in caring for pets, whatever their kind, ideas

These mice are enjoying a treat of seeds (in spray form). Many kinds of seeds have a high fat content, so feed them in moderate amounts.

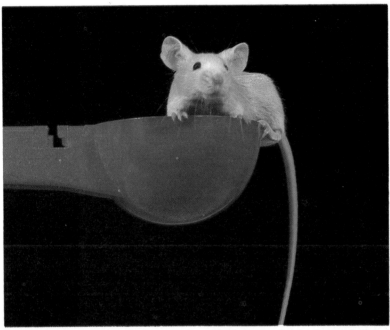

By nature, mice generally do not "pig out." If given a food mix consisting of various items, they will often sort through it for their favorite, and leave the remainder untouched.

disagree as to exactly what to feed individual mice. Pet owners have one set of ideas while the professional fancier has another.

Most fanciers feed a basic bulk diet of grain and bread soaked in water, the bulk of the grain mixture being whole or crushed oats and small (i.e., one to ten) parts of wheat or maize flakes. In cold weather the ratio can be raised to one in four parts. The bread, preferably whole meal, should be thoroughly stale and of course free of any mold or mustiness. This is then soaked in cold water for about 10-15 minutes; all excess water is then squeezed out. It can then be fed as it is or can be mixed with additives such as cod liver oil, wheat germ or milk. All the oils tend to be highly concentrated, so only a few

Feeding

Pet mice will eat a variety of foods. Whatever items you choose to include in your mouse's diet, make sure they are of the freshest quality.

drops need be added.

Many fanciers have an established menu for feeding, for example:

Day one: bread mixed with wheat bran.

Day two and three: bread mixed with bran and milk.

Day four: bread mix and wheat germ oil.

Day five and six: bread and bran mix.

Day seven: bread and bran mixed with an egg yolk.

Day eight and nine: bread and bran.

Then back to day one.

Each day grain is fed.

The bread should be damp and crumbly, not soggy and any left over from the previous feed should be removed or it will go sour and cause upset stomachs. Some fanciers give water while others do not, relying on moisture from the wet bread and additional vegetables, for example carrots or rutabagas. I personally prefer to give water in bottles.

Hay as a food is often forgotten. Only the best available should be used. Hay contains the ingestible fibers which hold the feces together and is a good conditioner.

With this diet, I would also suggest that a hard dog biscuit be placed in each cage. This good for the teeth and also helps prevent the animals' chewing the cage.

Some fanciers prefer a simpler diet, although it must be said mice do often get fat on this mixture if overfed. This diet contains a grain mixture as a basic, with the addition of vegetable and fruit.

The basic seed mixture should consist of the following grains in these proportions: Wheat, 10%; Crushed Oats, 20%; Barley, 5%; Buckwheat, 5%; Corn, 10%; Rice (natural),

10%; Millet, 15%; Canary seed, 10%; Grass seed, 10%; Sunflower, 1%; Hemp, 1%; Linseed, 2%; Peanuts, 1%.

To this I would also add a few dog biscuits, either broken oe whole.

In addition to these grains and seeds, mice enjoy greens and fruits. My own mice love tender fresh grass for example. They don't always eat it all but just nibble at the sweet ends. Other favorites are lettuce, endive, Brussel sprouts, curly kale, dandelions, carrots, pears, grapes,

You can offer your mouse treat foods that are tasty and nutritious. With the wide variety of commercial foods that are available for small animals such as mice, there is no reason for your pet to have a boring diet. Photo courtesy Vitakraft.

cucumbers, dates, figs, raisins, strawberries, and bean shoots.

Wild mice will occasionally grab and eat a worm or an insect such as a caterpillar. Mice in captivity take a wide range of foods: minced meat, mealworms, cheese or hard boiled eggs, cooked chicken, or beef heart.

HOW MUCH TO FEED?

Each feeding should consist of about 8-10 grams (.28-.35 oz.) of food per animal.

Healthy mice will not usually gorge themselves but will dig out large amounts of feed to rummage through for their favorite tidbits. It is difficult to advise on weights and amounts of vegetable. Generally, mice take only very small portions of vegetables, and you will be the best judge of the amount of each type of food to give. In my opinion water should always be available in a water bottle.

Normal-coated and rex-coated mice.

Opposite: *The more you handle your pet, the more accustomed he will be to your presence.*

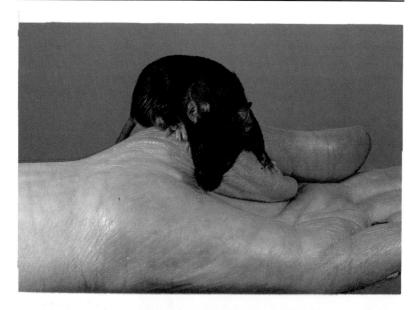

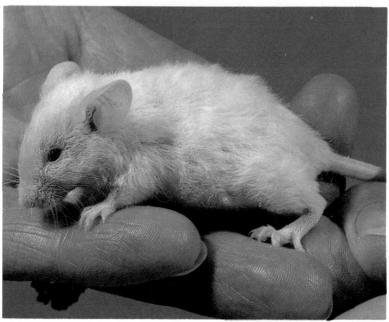

AILMENTS AND HEALTH

One of the most important factors in retaining a stock of any captive species is good hygiene. Prevention is infinitely better than cure. A basic understanding of hygiene will considerably reduce the risks of disease affecting your animals. There are two basic groups of diseases.

A. Communicable: those caused by disease organisms that are transmitted from one animal to another and

B. Non-communicable: those caused by other factors such as physical injury, malnutrition, and chemical poisoning.

It is, of course, easier to prevent conditions of the latter type, as sensible husbandry is all that is required.

It is not always an easy matter to diagnose a disease in a sick mouse, although signs of ill health are usually obvious. Always inspect your stock daily and watch for signs of disease; a vigilant owner will

Good management and adherence to basic hygienic practices will go a long way in keeping your mouse healthy.

If you have to handle a sick mouse, be sure to wash your hands afterwards.

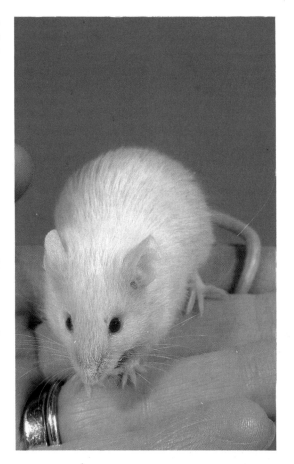

soon nip any signs of trouble in the bud and save himself an awful lot of worry later on. Distinct signs of ill health include diarrhea, sneezing, wheezing, runny nose, hunched-up appearance, scruffy coat, and general lethargy. These signs are not all likely to occur at the same time, but each one or combination of them are indicative of a specific disease or ailment. Never handle a fit animal after handling an ill one; deal with healthy animals first, then sick ones—*then* wash your hands thoroughly.

The following are some of the more common ailments found in mice. But don't worry; if your hygienic principles are sound, you are most unlikely to be troubled by any of them. Also remember, if you are in doubt at all, please consult your vet.

Abscesses: These are usually caused by infection entering through a small

This page and opposite: *The more familiar you are with your mouse's behavior, the easier it will be to discern when he is not feeling well.*

wound often caused by fighting. The abscess usually appears as a soft lump under the fur. Such lumps will gradually increase in size and eventually burst with a discharge. When this finally happens, the remaining pus should be gently squeezed out and the wound bathed with an antiseptic solution in warm water. Continue to bathe daily until the wound begins to heal. In some severe cases it may well be necessary to take the animal to the vet for antibiotic treatment.

Asthma: Strangely enough, this is fairly common in mice. It is usually attributed to an allergic reaction to dust, particularly from hay that is slightly moldy.

Bloat: Sudden changes in feed or an excess of fresh vegetables or fruit will cause this condition. Treat by adjusting the diet.

Coccidiosis: This is a very unpleasant disease that is also very infectious, as it is easily spread via the feces of infected animals. If caught in early stages, it is treatable with antibiotics. The cage (and

Nestled in the palm of its owner's hand, this fancy mouse gives evidence of its trusting nature.

items in the cage) of an infected animal must be thoroughly cleaned and disinfected.

Constipation: Rare in mice. Should it occur give the animal a couple of drops of liquid paraffin or castor oil orally via an eye dropper and recovery is usually rapid. To prevent this reoccurring, adjust the diet and provide more green foods.

Diarrhea: A symptom of many different diseases and conditions. The simplest cause is too much green foods or fruit. Cut out all fresh foods and seek the advice of your vet. This is also a symptom of coccidiosis so do please be careful.

Ectoparasites: Small creatures of several types which live either in the body of the mouse or in nooks and crannies in and around the cage. Mites are particularly nasty and will cause loss of fur and encrustation of the skin. Other blood-sucking parasites, such as lice, can be killed by dusting animals and the insides of the cages with special dusting powders that may be obtained from your vet or pet shop.

Fits: Occasionally, a mouse may be prone to fits. For no apparent reason it will suddenly start dashing around in circles for several minutes before collapsing from exhaustion. Such mice are usually incurable and it is best to cull them.

Foot and Tail Rot: An unpleasant condition that is usually caused by *streptobacillus* infection of the skin, usually on the tail or feet, where it manifests itself as a small sore that develops into a large encrusted area. This disease is extremely infectious and a killer, but it does respond well to antibiotic treatment if caught in its early stages.

Hypothermia: The lowering of normal body temperature usually caused by cold, wet conditions and/or a poor diet. Warm mice up by cupping them in the hands or placing them near a source of heat.

Middle or Inner Ear Disease: This condition is caused by an infection of the inner ear and results in the delicate balance mechanism being disturbed. Infected mice will lean to one side and walk around in circles. Usually there is no cure.

BUYING MICE

Naturally your first step will be a pet shop. If you don't see the particular variety that you want, perhaps the dealer can order it for you.

WHAT TO CHOOSE?

First of all, choose young, immature animals. Mice, you must remember, have a very short life span; they usually live for only $1\frac{1}{2}$ to $3\frac{1}{2}$ years, although 7 years has been recorded. Young mice will get used to you and become tame a lot faster. Look at your mice very carefully to be sure that none of them are diseased. Healthy mice have clear alert eyes and are very mobile and

Your most important consideration in selecting a mouse is to choose an animal that is sound and healthy. The color and "look" of your prospective pet is secondary.

Never try to catch your pet by restricting him with any type of container, as doing so might injure him. Instead, gently cup your hands around his body.

slim. The fur color of young animals is more intense, more glossy than that of older ones; ears are more delicate and show a little more hair. In short, when choosing a mouse keep the following in mind:

1. The animal should be neither too fat nor too skinny.

2. The back should not be arched or the fur shaggy.

3. There should be no bald patches on the coat.

4. The anal area should be clean.

COMING HOME

When you get your animal home, it will probably be frightened from its trip. You should place it into its new home, which you should have made ready before you went to collect your animal. Then just leave your animal alone for awhile. I know that this can be difficult but it is for the best. Once in its new home, it will probably take cover in its bedding and from there it will explore its new surroundings.

Buying Mice

Once it has had the chance to do this for awhile, you may approach the cage and put your hand inside to get the mouse used to the way you smell. To avoid scaring it too much, it is very important not to make any sudden moves. The hand you offer should be especially still, for the mouse to sniff at. In a short time, you can move your hand and touch or pick up your mouse.

TAMING

I feel that it takes a couple of days for a mouse to get used to its new surroundings. As soon as you have started to touch your mouse without its running away into its nest, you can begin to really train it. Try placing food on the palm of your hand and allow the mouse to climb on the palm of your hand to eat or collect the food. It is sometimes best to not feed your animal for the day until you put the food in your palm. Usually it doesn't take long at all for the mouse to decide that you will not harm it. Once the animal starts to take food from your hand, you can really start stroking it rather than just touching it. Picking up a mouse that isn't completely tame is a difficult thing at times. For a start, you have to get hold of it first. Any awkward handling can be painful both for the mouse and yourself if it decides to bite. Mice can safely be held by holding the *base* of the tail firmly and placing the mouse on the palm of the other hand or the other arm. However, a really tame mouse may be held in cupped hands or even allowed to climb all over you!

Opposite: *Mice are notably undemanding pets. Following the rules of good mouse care can help to ensure a healthy, contented pet.*

BREEDING

House or fancy mice reach sexual maturity and are thus able to breed at approximately 12 weeks of age, although I have known animals breeding at five weeks. For the best results for both adults and young animals, mice should not be allowed to breed before at least 16 weeks of age. Although males may be ·used at 10 weeks old, they should not be over-used. If you have a really super stud buck (male) who continually turns out decent young, he can be used until he grows visibly old and loses his virility. Does

Mice mating. A successful breeding program begins with the selection of the best stock possible.

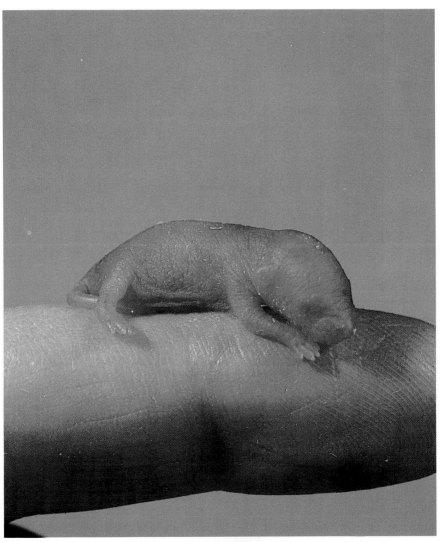

A six-hour-old mouse. Newly born mice are hairless and blind and completely helpless.

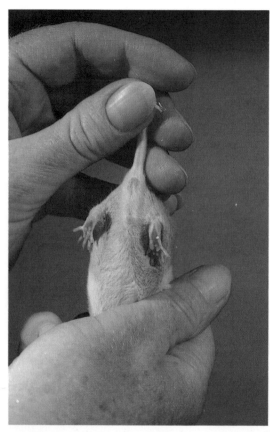

A male mouse. Sexing mice is not particularly difficult, even when the animals are quite young.

the buck and the doe together you can guess fairly accurately when litters will be due because mating will occur almost immediately. The gestation or period of pregnancy lasts for between 18 and 21 days. By the 14th day it will be very obvious that your doe is pregnant, and it is at this point that

(females), on the other hand, should not be overbred. Older does cannot produce as much milk as younger ones, for example. Most animals are at their best, in breeding terms, with their second litter. Each female comes into heat over a period of four to six days and the period lasts for about 12 hours or so. Once you place

the buck should be removed. I tend to let two or three does kindle (give birth) together. In this situation they will happily suckle each other's litter in a communal nest. It is, however, important that they kindle within a day or two of each other; otherwise the last born will have to fight the older and stronger ones for the food. I prefer to have only two does together; this helps if one is a bad mother or doesn't have enough milk and also one can keep the litter warm while the other is away from the nest for whatever reason.

After removing the buck, he should not be left alone, particularly if he is to be used as a show animal. If left alone for more than a day or two he will lose condition. Nor can he be placed with other bucks: he should be placed into a fresh box with new does. Always pair mice up in a cage new to all the individuals; otherwise you may find that those that occupy the cage will attack the

intruder into their territory.

Do not handle pregnant does, if at all possible, during the last few days of pregnancy. Make sure that they receive extra bedding and plenty of food, especially vitamins. When the litter has been born, carefully inspect the nest and dispose of any stillborn babies. The litter may number as few

A female mouse.

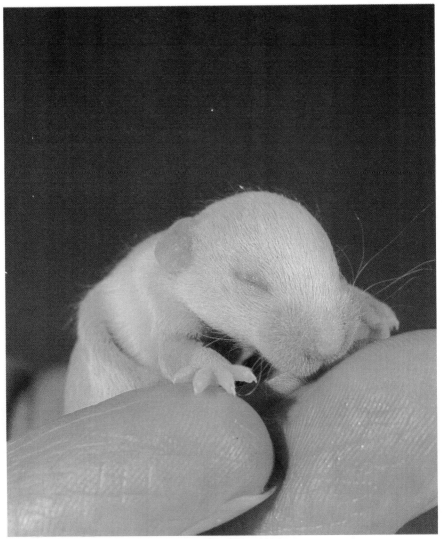

A ten-day-old mouse. Note the length of its whiskers.

An adult mouse and its baby. Newborn mice are completely reliant upon their mothers for nurturance.

as one or two or as many as eighteen; an ideal litter size is eight. Too few may indicate low fertility; too many and they will be very small and may not develop into big adults. You can take the doe out while you inspect the nest, but if the doe is friendly, this should not really be necessary. It is, however, wise to rub your fingers in a soiled corner of the cage so that you have the mother's scent on you when touching the babies.

Newborn mice are completely helpless creatures, naked and blind. So they have to rely entirely on the mother's milk to survive. Fanciers tend

This mouse litter is one day old. A litter size averages between eight and ten, but litters as small as one and as large as eighteen have been recorded.

to cull all babies with the exception of three or four to ensure that both babies and the mother remain as healthy as possible. The litter should be left alone for three or four days. Then the runts of the litter should be culled out; then cull out any with damaged tails or feet. The hair begins to grow after a few days so that color and any markings may be seen. Further culling should take place with any that are mismarked or of poor color. This should be done gradually. About ten days later, there should only be three or four babies left. It is due to the fact that this culling process has been used so widely over the years that show mice are so exceptional of both size and fitness. In fact, one or two people I have met refuse to believe that 'normal' pet mice and show mice are the same species. Culling should be thought of not as destroying life but as helping the stronger to survive better. Culling can also be useful for keeping down the numbers of males, as a breeder will not require very many males at all. It is not difficult, with a little experience, to sex even newborn animals. Mice can mate at five weeks

The swollen appearance of this female clearly indicates that she will soon give birth. The gestation period for mice is between 18 and 21 days.

and for this reason the young bucks should be separated from both their mother and sisters at 21-27 days. Young mice should be handled

Mice develop at a remarkable rate. This seven-day-old specimen already exhibits well-defined claws.

frequently from a very young age until they are six to seven weeks old and ready for breeding.

FOSTERING

At some time or another it may well be necessary for a breeder to foster part or a whole litter from one doe to another. Fostering can be useful during breeding operations if, for example, you have a very exceptional doe from whom you require the maximum number of litters. Thus, some, or even all, of her young may be fostered to other proven brood does. In this way there is no danger of culling what may at a later date prove to be a champion. However, I would still advise that the runts be culled as normal. If you relieve a doe of her litter and give her a week or so of rest, she may then be remated to a different buck and the process continued.

Foster does should be mated at the same time as the "exceptional" doe. Once all the does have given birth, the mother should be removed while the changeover takes place. Gently rub each baby with a little of the foster mother's soiled litter so that she cannot detect a strange scent. The foster mother can then be placed in the cage and given something to eat. In most cases, there should be no trouble whatsoever. Another method of fostering is to first mate your good does and then mate a foster doe a day or two later. The foster mother will litter later than the "exceptional" so you can easily recognize the different litters, the foster doe's litter being the smaller individuals.

Shorthaired and Longhaired mice. The Longhaired mouse is a relative newcomer to the mouse fancy.

A mother mouse and her mouselings. After a litter is born, the nest should be inspected and any dead animals should be removed and disposed of.

COLORS AND VARIETIES

Most colors and varieties of fancy mouse have arisen from the development of mice bred in laboratories at the end of the 19th century.

As mentioned in the introduction, there is almost an infinite number of colors and varieties of fancy mouse with new colors and forms constantly being developed. It is therefore impossible to mention all of them in this book. However, I shall describe a broad section of the types most commonly seen.

When showing a mouse, each individual should have a particular general appearance as laid down by the governing body of the fancy. In the US, this is the American Fancy Rat

One of the most exciting aspects of the mouse fancy is the ongoing development of new varieties and colors.

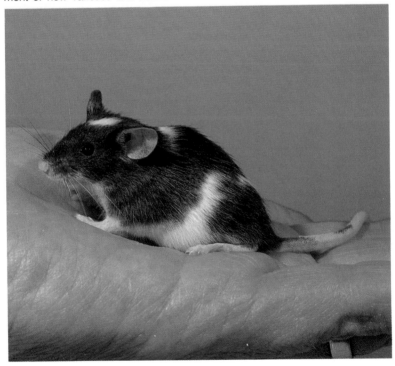

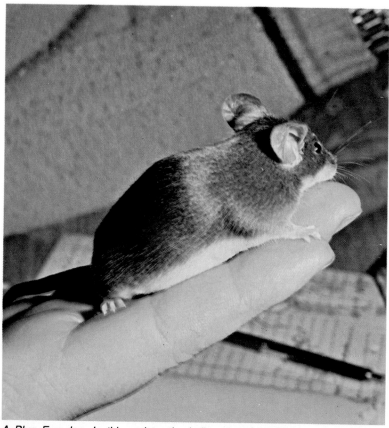

A *Blue Fox doe. In this variety, the belly color should be as near white as possible.*

and Mouse Association. In the UK this is the National Mouse Club.

Generally each mouse must be long in the body with a long head; it should not be too fine nor pointed towards the nose.

The eyes should be large and prominent. The ears should also be large and tulip-shaped, free from creases. They should be carried erect with plenty of width between them. The body should be slim, with a slight arch over the loin. The tail should be free from kinks and come out well of the back, thick at the base and gradually tapering to the tip. The length should be equal to that of the head and body. The coat should be short and perfectly smooth unless otherwise stated in the standard. The mouse should be free from any deformity at all. Nor should it have any sores, bald patches, cuts, bad eyes, missing toes, etc.

The colors or mutations of

Mice of the Tan variety are so named for the attractive golden-reddish tan color of their bellies.

Colors and Varieties

fancy mouse may be roughly divided into four categories as follows:—Selfs, Tans, Marked, and Any Other Variety (AOV). However, before going into the details of the colors and varieties themselves, it is important to have some basic idea of genetics and recessive inheritance is indicated in respect of a mutation when the color disappears in crosses with the original wild color (Agouti). For example, when an Agouti is mated to a Pink Eyed White, the youngsters that result are all Agouti in color, similar to

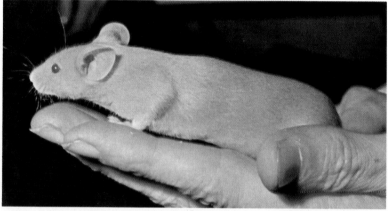

If your mouse is to be a show animal, it will have to become accustomed to being handled. The more you handle him at home, the more comfortable he will be when he is being held by a judge at a show.

understanding of some of the words mentioned—for example, the difference between dominant and recessive.

Dominant and recessive are the two forms of inheritance, the recessive being the most common form.

It may be assumed that a the Agouti parent. This proves that Agouti is dominant to Pink Eyed White and that Pink Eyed White is recessive to Agouti. The youngsters, if mated together, will give young of both Agouti and Pink Eyed White in the proportion of 75% and 25% respectively. However, should you mate them back to the Pink Eyed White parent, the proportion changes to 50% Agouti and 50% Pink Eyed White.

This shows what is known as the typical 3:1 ratio which plays an important part in genetics. The fact that the Pink Eyed White color does not reappear until the second generation need not worry the breeder because once it has recurred, the Pink Eyed White youngsters are true breeding and will not revert to Agouti if mated together. The first cross of any two colors is known as the F1 generation and when these are mated together produce the F2 generation. A dominant form of inheritance is indicated in respect of a mutation when a color does not disappear in crosses with the normal Agouti.

One point to remember is

A Sable mouse. This mouse's very glossy coat makes it particularly attractive.

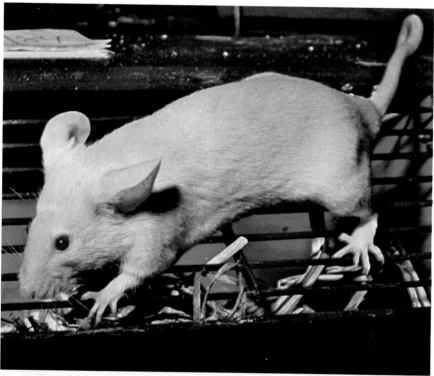

A Self Champagne mouse. If you are going to let your mouse out of his cage for additional exercise, you should closely supervise him to prevent his being injured or harmed.

that whether one is dealing with either a dominant or a recessive inheritance, the color is not necessarily lost if not seen. Because an individual does not appear to be Agouti or whatever, this is in fact not always the case. The facts are that more likely than not it is split or a carrier of one or more colors. For example, if a split Agouti was mated to a Pink Eyed White and produced a litter of three Agouti and one Pink Eyed White, then it can be assumed that the Agouti is split for, or a carrier of, Pink Eyed White. A split animal can be recognized by a number of means. If an individual produces more than one color type among its offspring then it is certainly a split animal, so that if an Agouti mated to a Pink Eyed White, the young, although appearing Agouti, are in fact split for Pink Eyed White. When two different color varieties are mated together it is certain that the youngsters will be split animals of one type or another, and one can assume that the offspring will be split for the color that has disappeared.

STANDARDS

Written standards for all small livestock—not only

A Golden Agouti. In length, a mouse's tail should be equal to the length of its body.

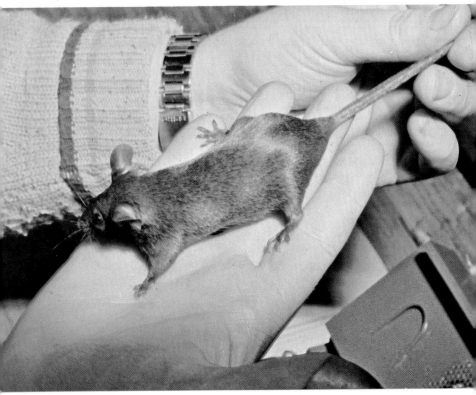

mice—are necessarily
deficient for words; especially,
the written words cannot
convey an exact idea of what
any given variety should look
like. For this reason I would
suggest that anyone wishing to
form an opinion on a given
color or variety should attend a
number of top shows. Nothing
really can take the place of
firsthand inspection of good
show animals. However,

having said all this, the written
standards do give a general
idea of what you should expect
to see.

THE SELFS

Selfs are recognized in the
following colors: White, black,
blue, chocolate, cream,
champagne, silver, dove, red,
and fawn. Of these, three
colors are recognized with
both black and pink eyes,

Seal Point mouse. Your pet's show accommodations should be clean and comfortable.

A Fawn Satin mouse. The items that you use to house and to transport your mouse must allow for adequate ventilation.

these being white, cream, and silver. "Self" means that the color should be the same color on whatever part of the body it occurs in a very even color. It is this point that is the most difficult to perfect, and this is particularly true of the belly color. The reason for this is that the fur of the belly is not as dense as that of the top coat. This slight fault is usually allowed for to some extent. But obviously, when selecting matings, all mice with thin belly fur should be discarded if at all possible. One or other of the selfs are, generally speaking, most recommended for the new fancier, providing good

Colors and Varieties

The Chinchilla mouse's coat color resembles that of the chinchilla. It is a delicate shade of pearl gray with a slate blue undercolor.

foundation stock can be obtained.

So let's look at the Self colors in detail.

Pink Eyed White. Probably *the* color in the fancy mouse. It is usually excellent in type and size and low in faults. It is a valuable outcross, and because of this most fanciers carry a stock of this variety, if only for improving other varieties. Occasionally other colors push the PE White from the top spot but it always appears to eventually bounce back.

Black Eyed White. The Black Eyed White is very far removed from the Pink Eyed White, the reason being that while the PE White is an albino, the BE White is actually a pied mouse with no markings except for the color of the eye itself.

Black Eyed Whites are difficult to breed and generally are far inferior to PE White in both size and type. A large proportion of marked animals often turn up in the litters of Black Eyed Whites. The most successful mating appears to be mating the lightest marked

a beautiful animal to behold; black always appear to reflect good condition and care better than any other color. Naturally, the color should be a dense lustrous one. It is a very popular color; thus competition is keen. A single colored hair or nail on an otherwise perfect animal would prevent a black from winning any award. So

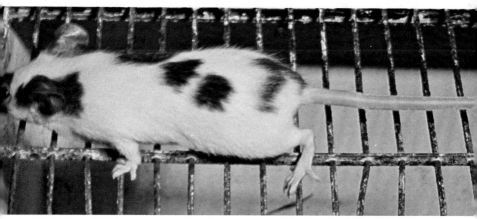

This distinctively patterned mouse is known as a Broken. In show mice, the patches of color are evaluated for their clarity of color.

doe to the purest colored buck; this should give a fair percentage of clear white young.

Black. Well, to be honest, the Black speaks for itself. A top class black is, to my mind,

any animal showing this fault should, if at all possible, not be bred from.

Most breeders breed only black to black; however some will occasionally try an outcross to another color to improve size and type points

Colors and Varieties

on which blacks sometimes fall down. One of the best for this is Blue; in fact many fanciers keep both Blacks and Blues in their studs, crossing each with the other when desired. A couple of the best blue does should be mated to your best black buck. From the resulting litter, which will be entirely black—the blue being a dilute gene of black—keep only does and mate these back to a black buck. Sadly, feet will suffer for a couple of

generations. Only introduce into your black stud when you are sure you have perfected the faults. Other breeders outcross to PE white or some other colors. These can be successful, but try to avoid Champagne or Chocolate, as with these a rusty tinge will begin to appear.

Blue. The Blue in the mouse is a slate blue. It is not as popular as the closely related Black. Blues on the whole tend to suffer from a number of faults; tan vent, light feet, white or colored hairs in the coat. It is also difficult to produce the medium shade required by the standard. In litters, light, medium, and dark shades will appear and these must be blended to produce the ideal animal. The blue dilution

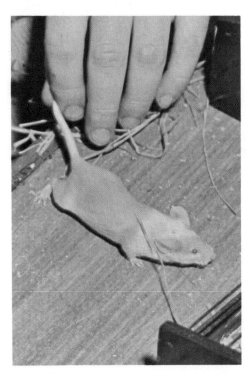

An especially pretty color variety of mouse is the Self Dove. Mice of this variety possess a dove-gray coat that complements their pink eyes.

This curious little fellow is a Chocolate White Rump mouse. The line of demarcation between the rump and the rest of the body should be clearly defined and even.

factor tends to create a distinctly ticked or clumpy appearance in the lighter shade, which is totally undesirable. If the top color or the feet are too light, then it may be worth outcrossing to a self Black.

Chocolate. The Chocolate talked about in the mouse fancy is that of plain (not milk) chocolate, rich and deep. Sadly, as I like this variety, it has few devotees and is rarely seen. They do tend to suffer from tan vents and throat spots, as well as tan hairs along the flanks and particularly around the teats of the does.

The only sensible outcross

If you think you would like to pursue color breeding, you should familiarize yourself with the basic fundamentals of genetics.

for the Chocolate is the self black in order to darken the coat color. Since black is dominant to chocolate, all the first generation will be black and these mice should either be mated together or back to a chocolate. Select only the very best to breed with. Chocolates are not difficult to breed but it will take a lot of patience and devotion to succeed.

Cream—Black and Pink Eyed. A pale cream, difficult to describe exactly but it should not be confused with ivory, stone or even dilute champagne.

I am told that the early creams were difficult to produce as then they were the production of Red to Blue, but modern Creams have been produced by chinchillating the

Self Chocolate. The cream is often recommended to the beginner, although competition is strong in this color.

You can outcross to PE White and winners can immediately result from such a cross. However, any PE babies from such a cross should not be used for breeding PE Whites. The white outcrosses should not be resorted to too often or belly color will suffer and become far too pale.

Many dark shades of

Some mice are better "beginner's mice" than others. Your pet shop dealer can provide you with the information that you need to make the wisest selection.

This cluster of mice illustrates that in the world of animal acrobats, mice are notable performers.

beigeish or even lilac can and do crop up when breeding cream and it is important not to destroy all of these. Constant breeding together: mate those too dark to those too light and the correct shade will be produced.

The Pink Eyed Cream is very rare indeed!!!

Champagne. The standard quotes this color as being of "Champagne silk with a pinkish tinge." A difficult color to describe, it really has to be seen at shows, but once seen it is never forgotten. An attractive color and it is one of the most popular. Genetically, the Champagne is a pink eyed Chocolate. Various shades have to be used to create the correct show shade. Breeders blend light, medium, and dark shades and any super-light or pale animals are discarded along with those that are very dark. If after repeated Champagne to Champagne matings litters are too dark, introduce a self Silver outcross.

Silver—Black and Pink Eyed. A delicate shade as near to an old silver coin as possible. There are, however, many, many shades of silver— from off white to light dove. As the Champagne is a PE Chocolate, the Silver is a PE Blue, although strictly speaking, the Silver is not a self as each hair contains more pigment at the base. However, this should really only be evident when the coat is blown back and a bluish undercolor is seen and without which it would be a rather drab color. It is also questionable as to whether a Pink Eyed Silver is genetically possible.

The self silver is like all the delicate shades that the breeder must balance his breeding program to allow for. It is generally regarded as the best outcross for the Pink Eyed White, since Pink Eyed Whites so bred can be very useful for improving other varieties and make good foster mothers.

Dove. The Dove was the color that really won me over to mice, a beautiful soft dove gray. It was also the most recent addition to the standards of the selfs. It was originally the result of crossing Champagnes with Blacks, then mating the resulting blacks together, thus making the Dove genetically a pink eyed Black. It is genetically akin to silver. An excellent outcross for improving size and type is thus readily available. It is also easier to produce Doves by mating Silver and Champagne

rather than Champagne and Black, with Doves appearing in the first litter.

Red. A beautiful rich deep color that really is difficult to describe but again, once seen, never ever forgotten. Sadly,

Mice are noted for their remarkable ability to adapt to a number of varied habitats.

Colors and Varieties

A Longhaired mouse. Ideally, the body of a mouse should be long and slim in appearance.

for this purpose is the Golden Agouti or Cinnamon.

Most breeders of Red maintain that the Cinnamon cross gives the best results, while the Agouti tends to make them too sooty in color. The Reds crossed to Cinnamon would give approximately equal numbers of each in the litters and it is then up to the individual breeder as to how to progress. Possibly an even better outcross would be the Cinnamon Tan, as the tan factor would deepen the belly color.

this is very definitely *not* a color for a beginner. Reds have a tendency to obesity and continual breeding of Red to Red will produce, small, fat poor type animals with short tails and small ears. Thus to counteract all this, an outcross is required. Over the years it has been found that the best

As they put on weight so

easily, Reds must be fed with special care; do not overfeed them. If they get fat, they will more than likely not breed. Many fanciers have advised breeding Reds from an early age, say ten weeks, and not letting them rest between litters. Foster mothers have a part to play in this.

Fawn. A deep tan rather than fawn—almost a deep orange. Probably *the* most attractive of all the mouse colors. It is the Pink Eyed Red. Although related to it, it doesn't have the problems of the Red.

The Fawn has a super natural outcross in the Champagne tan, and this outcross will improve size, type, and small ears, areas that the Fawns can fall down on. It also helps with the belly color. It should not, however, be undertaken too often or the top color will pale too much. It is probably best to pick a Champagne Tan that is too dark a Champagne. Do not use any Tans produced to breed back to Tans however. Once size and type are

A mouse of the Rex variety. Rex-type mice exhibit a coat that is noticeably wavy in appearance.

Colors and Varieties

established, Fawn-to-Fawn breeding can be undertaken.

THE TANS

As a whole, the Tan section is the most popular and all the Tan varieties can be recommended to the beginner. Tans are recognized in any standard color and the top color shall be as that of the recognized colors. There should be a clear line of demarcation between the top color and the tan belly, with the line running along the flanks, chest, and on the jaw; there should be no brindling or guard hairs. The feet should be the color of top color and never tan.

Although Tans are recognized in any standard color, it is not genetically possible to tan each and every color. For example, is it is impossible to tan Red or fawn, as these already have Tan bellies.

The six most popular Tans at shows today are; Black, Blue, Chocolate, Champagne, Silver, and Dove. From time to time Pearl, Cinnamon, and Agouti Tans also appear.

It is fairly easy to maintain the top color in Tans along with the fiery depth of Tan color. The greatest problem with Tans is to maintain a rich tan without letting it spread to places where it is not required—for example, around the base of the tail, behind the ears and the feet.

An ideal Tan would be one that when viewed from above could be mistaken for a self and only when held up reveals the Tan belly. The way to breed Tan is to keep some of the mice that, if shown, would be sent off the bench for lack of depth of color in the Tan. If you persist in mating the richest Tan to the richest Tan, the color will spread. A more drastic method is to mate a Tan to a self of the equivalent top color. However, this usually means a delay of three or four generations before the tan is rich once again. Selfs from these crosses should not be mated back to a self line.

Black Tan. The Black Tan is one, if not *the,* most popular of the Tans, I assume because of the striking contrast between the two colors. Black Tan to Black Tan appears to be the most desirable mating, if only the best are selected at all times. Some breeders use a Blue Tan outcross; strangely

A Rex mouse. Note the prominent vibrissae (whiskers), which are an important sensory device of the mouse.

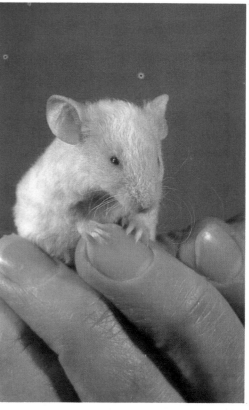

the Black Tan often lacks size and bone when compared to the other Tans.

Chocolate Tan. The ideal outcross for Chocolate is the Black Tan, which should improve both top and belly color. Due to the lack of bone in Black Tans, only good Black Tans should be used.

Blue Tan. The Blue Tan is the most controversial of all the Tans. You either love them or hate them. The problem with the Blue Tan is that its belly color is nowhere near the same depth as that of the other Tans. The reason for this is that blue is a dilute and has the effect on the belly of reducing color to a light buff. However, generally allowance is made for this and it is judged accordingly.

Champagne Tan. This is quite a subtle combination of colors that I personally cannot decide if I like or not. There are no serious problems in breeding this variety although the breeder really must be skilled to achieve the required

Colors and Varieties

Hide and seek—mouse style. Pet shops stock a variety of devices that will provide your pet with ample opportunity for exercise.

pinkish shade of the top color combined to the rich tan.

Silver and Dove Tans.
These two are often bred in conjunction with each other and are my favorites in the Tan group.

The Dove Tan has the strongest Tan of all the pink eyed Tans and is the easiest to breed. While the top color may be perfected through continuous breeding of Silver Tan to Silver Tan, the tan will grow progressively weaker. Yet by using the Dove Tans occasionally, the strength of the tan can be maintained. Conversely, the Silver can help the Dove by not allowing the top color of the latter to become too dark. Be careful, however, as light nose will occur with alarming frequency.

MARKED
The Marked section consists of only six varieties, namely: Dutch, Broken, Evens, Himalayans, Rump White, Variegated. A small section? Well, yes and no; although

small in varieties, it is numerically very strong.

The Piebald Mouse:
Namely the Dutch and Broken. These appear to hold the greatest attraction for newcomers. The appeal, I assume, lies not only in the beauty of the marked animal but also in the belief that it is easier to choose from his stock the animals with the most show potential, rather than to decide, for instance, between different shades in a self. This may be true to some extent; the beginner who is initially confused by the countless different colors will soon be able to recognize the correct shades. I have seen many a beginner become very disillusioned when starting with

marked varieties, and I would advise against these as a starter. Nothing is more disheartening than lack of success. Whereas one can expect exhibition quality, if not actual winners, in most litters of Self or Tans or even AOV, with marked, perhaps only one in a thousand is a winner.

Breeding to a selected pattern requires an abundance of patience and perseverance,

Mice are natural-born explorers that can spend hours investigating nooks and crannies.

Colors and Varieties

besides a knowledge of how to balance matings in an effort to produce the showable animal. If such an exceptional animal is produced, it is certainly worth more than any other variety.

A good marked mouse will last longer on the show bench. Many breeders of marked varieties believe that the main advantage is that by the age of three or four days, any mismarked babies can be seen and destroyed. In other groups this culling is a gamble; not so with the marked. Size, type, and stamina are generally not so good in the marked. The reason for this is that the best marked animals are kept even if they are the runts of the litter, and extremely close inbreeding is required to retain all the good points of the strain.

An exercise wheel is a special favorite with mice. Like all other cage accessories, toys should be cleaned on a regular basis.

No matter what color or variety of mouse you choose, your new little friend is sure to entertain you with his humorous antics.

Dutch. The Dutch is probably *the* most popular of this section and one of the most popular of all mouse varieties. Dutch markings are well-known to all breeders of small livestock, as they also occur in the rabbit and the cavy. It is quite difficult to explain a Dutch-marked animal to someone who has never seen one. Basically, the markings are on a white animal, the colored markings being the color of any recognized color. The face or cheek markings should be evenly balanced, a patch covering each side of the face, extending from underneath the eye but not to include the whiskers and not to run further back than is necessary to include the ear and forming a wedge-shaped blaze from the nose, tapering to a fine point between the ears. The cheek markings should not run beneath the jaw. The saddle should come well up from the tail to the middle of the body and be clean cut, top and bottom. The stops on hind feet should come half way between tips of the toes and hock. The color of the markings should be carried out in the ears.

Although the breeder plays a part in producing the perfect Dutch-marked mouse, to a greater extent luck is the major factor. It has been found that the best way to be successful with this variety is to actually adopt a rigid plan of close inbreeding to fix all good points of the strain and breed out the imperfections. Because there are so many faults to eradicate, it may well take several years to build up a consistently winning strain. Most of the top breeders tend to adopt a linebreeding system whereby father is mated to daughter and mother to son. This plan cannot, however, be followed dogmatically for it may be that cousin to cousin would be better. Crossing two strains will produce winners, but not consistent winners. Unfortunately, the outcome of such close inbreeding is that the Dutch Mouse is the smallest of all the mouse varieties and somewhat cobby and stout in general appearance. This is allowed for on the show bench, but it should not mean that the animal should be lacking in either fitness or stamina.

Dutch do not generally make good mothers due to their small size and low milk yield. Thus most breeders tend to foster Dutch litters out to PE Whites.

Although the Dutch is recognized in any standard color, the most commonly seen are Black, Blue, Chocolate, Agouti, and Cinnamon. In theory, top color should be as good as the standard varieties, but in actual fact even the top color is often lacking in the Dutch. Thus it is important not to overlook this point.

Broken. Broken marked Mice are nearly as popular as the Dutch, and it is certainly as difficult to produce champions from them. There is no fixed pattern for breeding and no two brokens are exactly the same. The ideal broken would be a piebald mouse that has colored spots or patches placed irregularly all over the body. The spots or patches should be of similar size, and there must be a nose spot.

There is no mention in the standards as to the actual number of patches, except to say that the more, the better. The difficulty here is to maintain a balance between the spots and the background color. The nose spot, being the only one mentioned in the standard, must be present. This important spot should be on one side of the nose only and may or may not include the eye on that side. Brokens with full nose spots and those without any markings at all are not desired and should not be used for breeding. If the nose spot is on the left side, then ideally the right ear should be pigmented and vice versa. The positioning of all other spots on the body are left to the selection of the breeder. If, for example, a mouse was bare of spots on one side, it would be mated to a mouse that has spots down the opposite side. Even or symmetrical markings of any description should not be tolerated when breeding brokens.

Color is very important. The standard requires spots or patches of clean color having a neat clean-cut appearance. They must be sharply defined, not ragged or brindled. Again, the color may be any of the recognized standards.

If you do not possess unlimited patience, then I suggest you do not attempt to breed brokens.

Evens. The standard of the Even is one that is more open to individual interpretation than any other. Few breeders specialize in this variety. Any mice discarded from Broken breeders may be used to establish an Even strain. Thus, for breeding Even, choose those mice with a full nose spot, even ears, shoulder spots and a central spot at the root of the tail. This gives a basis of six spots or patches to work from, and with two or three more in the center of the body would complete an ideal pattern.

Variegated. Once a popular variety now sadly quite rare. Genetically it is closely related to the Black Eyed White and goes hand in hand in the appearance stakes.

The make-up of the Variegated is completely different from that of the Broken or the Even. No solid patches are required, except splashes of color distributed evenly all over the body. The splashes should not be clean-cut but rather ragged and brindled at the edges. The difficulty is producing an animal in which color is evenly distributed without solid patches appearing on the rump, near the root of the tail, or around each side of the head. A percentage of the selfs will turn up in litters, those most set in type should be retained and mated back to lightly marked Variegated. Again, any recognized color is permissible in this variety.

Himalayan. The Himalayan is a white animal with darker chocolate points: i.e., nose, ears, tail and feet.

It is of comparatively recent origin, being only about twenty years old and was produced by crossing Seal Point Siamese to PE White. This simple cross has made the Himalayan comparable in all-around shape and carriage to any mouse variety.

The main difficulty with this variety is to produce an animal with dense points and a pure white body, the problem being the denser the points, the less pure the white body becomes, especially around the rump. The points are expected to be a light chocolate rather than the dark chocolate of the self.

The Himalayan gene is rather an unusual one in that it is temperature sensitive, and the points of the mouse

become denser in cold conditions. This is not to say, however, that you should treat this variety any differently from any of the others. It is probably the easiest of the marked varieties for the beginners, as once a stud has been established, winners can be bred consistently.

Rump Whites. The Rump White has provided another useful addition to this section and a beautiful one at that. The Rump White is any standardized color having a white rump. The line of demarcation should be straight and encircle the body so that the lower third of the mouse, including the hind feet and tail, is completely white. The remaining color must be without any white at all.

It appears that the Rump White is dominant to Self, so type is easy to maintain in this variety, with the demarcation line not being easily lost. However, it is also easy to breed in white hairs and patches to the colored area and this should be avoided at all costs.

ANY OTHER VARIETY
This section caters to any

standardized variety that cannot be classified in any other section and is commonly known as AOV. Numerically, it is perhaps naturally the largest section, with some 18 varieties. Some of these are very popular and of high standards; others are of poor quality and others are very rare indeed. The ticked varieties are Golden and Silver Agouti, Cinnamon, Chinchilla, Silver Gray, Brown, Fawn, Pearl, Argente and Argente Cream. Shaded varieties are Sable, Marten Sable and Seal Point Siamese. The Silver Fox (in Black, Blue and Chocolate) is unique, as are the Astrex,

Longhaired, Satin and Rex— all coat mutations. Only the satin is not classified in AOV. Due to its great popularity it has now been given a section all of its own.

Golden Agouti and Cinnamon. I shall combine comments on these two varieties, as they are so

A mouse's head is long and clean in appearance, neither too blunt nor too pointed.

closely related, have a similar standard and are usually classified together. The standard states that the Agouti shall be a rich brown or golden hue with even dark or black ticking all throughout. The belly shall be golden brown, ticked as on top and the feet shall match the body in color and ticking. Eyes are black. Cinnamon shall be of a rich golden tan, lustrous in color and level throughout top and under, with rich brown ticking clearly defined. No black ticking. Again, the eyes are black.

The Agouti coat pattern is basically that which can be found in animals in the wild state. It is usually fairly nondescript in this state. However, selective breeding has greatly enriched the color. The coat consists of three colors: black, yellow, and chocolate. Each hair at its base is black followed by a bar of chocolate, and some hairs, but not all, are tipped with yellow. All the various color mutations are derived from these three colors. An essential point with regard to the "Golden" Agouti is determined by the amount of yellow pigment in the coat pattern. A direct cross between Agouti and Cinnamon usually produces poorly colored youngsters in the first generation, but when these crossbred young are mated back to Agoutis, brighter offspring should result.

Should the Agoutis be lacking in ticking, the black tan will correct this. Keep only does from this cross and mate to an Agouti buck. Tans will continue to crop up and these should be culled. It is easy to pick them out in the nest a few days after birth, as the demarcation lines along the flanks can be seen. This cross can also improve type and size, but it can also cause tan around the vent.

The Cinnamon is similar to the Agouti except that it has no black pigment. The absence of melanism makes the Cinnamon a naturally larger type mouse than the Agouti. The Cinnamon has warmth of color, being a rich tan mouse with evenly defined chocolate ticking throughout the top and bottom.

Belly color of both varieties should match the top color.

Silver Agouti. This beautiful variety is like the normal

Agouti except that the golden brown pigment of the normal Agouti is replaced by silver gray. It is a recent addition to the fancy; it should have a silver cast that is bright and clear and not bronzed in the slightest. *

It was created by crossing normal Agouti to Chinchilla. Sad to say, the Silver Agouti has not as yet proved popular, probably because it is so similar to the Chinchilla.

Chinchilla. Without a doubt the Chinchilla is one of the most important varieties in the history of the fancy mouse. The following have all been obtained by crossing other colors to the Chinchilla: Silver Agouti, Silver Fox, Argente Creame, and the Marten Sable. Some also believe that the Chinchilla had a part in the production of Pearls, but this cannot be proved.

It should be as near as possible to the color of a wild Chinchilla, a rodent from South America; a slate blue undercolor and intermediate shade of pearl gray. Hairs are evenly tipped with black, belly white. Some Chinchilla mice have a brown tinge and these should not be used for breeding. However, by far the worst problem with this variety is molt. No exhibition animal can succeed if the coat is in molt and the Chinchilla appears to molt more readily than any other variety.

It is, however, a good beginners' variety, although due to the molt a large stud is required to allow one to show regularly. Blacks or Blues provide the best outcrosses.

Silver Gray, Fawn or Brown. Really, the Silver Gray is the only one of these colors that you are likely to come across, with, unfortunately, both the Silver Fawn and the Silver Brown being virtually extinct.

The silvering factor in the Silver Gray is the result of four types of hairs intermixed: 1. all black, 2. all white, 3. black with white tips, and 4. black, gray and white banded. Interestingly, the silvered animal is genetically unique, as it carries the gene for partial albinism; i.e., white hairs.

When in the nest, the babies appear selfs, but by four to five weeks the silvering begins to come through and increases with age, with the face, rump, and feet being the

Colors and Varieties

last areas to silver. Many otherwise good silver grays suffer from dark extremities in that the nose, tail root, and feet are solid and have no ticking. The ideal required by most judges is a black mouse with sharply defined ticking with the black carried to the base of the hair. This however does tend to be more often than not blue-black rather than black. The most logical outcross is self black, but as silvering is recessive to selfs, the first generation of such a cross would give only blacks. Mate these back to a silver.

Pearls. The Pearl Mouse is closely related to the Silver Grays. It is a pale silver, shading to a whitish undercolor, each hair tipped with gray or black. Pearls may be produced by mating light-colored Silver Grays together, providing they have a whitish undercolor.

Argente. The Argente is an extremely attractive variety. Genetically the Argente is a pink eyed Golden Agouti. It is a blended shade of light fawn and silver. The undercolor to be blue as dark as possible in shade; the belly to be a golden fawn as similar to the top color as possible. It must be remembered that the Argente carries the Agouti coat pattern and, as with the Agouti, the color deepens with age!

Argente Creame. This color variety can be fairly easily produced by introducing the pink eyed dilution factor to the chinchilla through normal Argente, the latter basically being a pink eyed Chinchilla or in other words a Chinchillaed Argente. It is a blend of deep cream and silver. When mating the pink eyed dilution to chinchilla, the first generation will be golden Agoutis. Interbreeding these will produce full Argente Creame. It is similar to the Argente, but the light fawn is replaced by deep cream. Because of the Chinchilla factor, the belly color is diluted to pure white; it still however has the blue undercolor but this should be very pale.

Sables. A distinctive color that is shaded rather than ticked. In the past, light, medium, and dark shades were recognized, but now really only the dark variety is regarded on the show bench.

Mice enjoy the opportunity to explore their surroundings. This mouse is peering out of a unit that is part of a housing and entertainment structure.

It is a black eyed variety. The top color is a rich dark brown as dark as possible; the shading should be gradual from the dorsal to the belly. The belly should be a rich golden tan. There should be no line of demarcation nor any blotches, patches, ticking or streakiness. The sable can be a problem at times. Genetically, it is a member of the yellow group of colors and this group is very prone to obesity. This in turn can lead to infertility. The anemic lethal factor is also linked to this group, so that when two mice of this group are mated together, approximately 25% die before birth—what is known as pre-natal lethal. For this reason Sable litters are small in numbers. To overcome these difficulties, a selected outcross is the only answer. For this the most suitable is the Black Tan. Not only does this variety help to keep the top dark and the belly fiery, but it also helps improve size, vigor, and above all, type.

Colors and Varieties

Marten Sables. Basically the Marten Sable is a normal Sable whose belly is white instead of tan—a Sable with the Chinchilla factor. The top color is a dark sepia, shading off to a paler color on lower jaws, sides and flanks, blending to be gradual, belly white with white ticking on flanks and the rump.

Silver Fox. A good variety for the novice, it can be recognized in black, blue, and chocolate. Only the feet, sides, and rump are to be evenly ticked with white hairs and a pure white belly. Usually produced by mating the Chinchilla to Black Tan.

Seal Point Siamese. A beautiful variety, the official standard states that the body color should be a medium beige with shadings, gradually shaded over the saddle and hindquarters, merging gradually with the body color and being darkest at the tail root as seen in the Siamese cat. The belly should be as near as possible in color and shadings as the top. Seal points shall be present on muzzle, ears, feet, tail, and tail root. There should be no demarcation line but a merging. Eyes may be either ruby or black.

Astrex. Although a number of different rex-type coats are known in the mouse, only the Astrex is recognized at present.

An Astrex mouse should have a coat as curly as possible with equally curly whiskers. The color may be of any recognized color.

It is an incredible variety and one of my great favorites. Each hair of the mouse is altered to give the effect of curly waves throughout its coat. Even the whiskers are curled. The curliness is usually most pronounced before the animals are eight weeks of age. Then the coat tends to straighten out, although not always. Size, type, and general stamina can also be failings of this variety. It is recessive to normal coat.

Longhaired. The Longhaired is a recent mutation and addition to the fancy. Its standard states that the Longhaired mouse shall have a coat as long as possible, combined with density and silky texture. The color may be of any recognized variety. It suffers from faults similar to those of the Astrex in that individuals appear to be better as youngsters than as adults. But with increased breeding for longer fur, this is beginning to be less of a problem, with undoubtedly the best specimens being produced in white although in all colors the ears tend to be small.

Satin. This mouse is undoubtedly the most sensational mutation that there is. The satin coat gives even the most dull color a new lease on life. It should have a high sheen, resulting in an exquisite satin-like or metallic gloss. The color may be any standard one.

An appealing assortment of mice. Compared to other pets, mice are relatively easy to maintain.

OTHER SPECIES OF MICE

Although this book is primarily about the fancy mouse, there are many other species of mouse that are kept in captivity. I am often asked by owners of the fancy type what other more "unusual" species they can keep and where they can find out how to look after them. I therefore hope in this short chapter to give you a brief outline on the most commonly seen species and how to care for them.

THE WOOD AND YELLOW-NECKED MICE

Both the Wood and the Yellow-necked mouse are species native to Eurasia and both are retained in captivity for varying periods of time. Although I am not aware of totally captive-bred populations, stock are often offered for sale in various European countries. Both are slightly larger than the fancy mouse. To my mind they do not make very easy-to-keep pets, as they are rather jumpy and nervous and rather prone to biting. They do not appear to calm down and adapt to captivity very well, even after a couple of generations of captive breeding. They are, however, quite capable of being very interesting pets for the dedicated few.

The Yellow-necked mouse (*Apodemus flavicollis*) has a head and body length of about 100mm, with a tail of an additional 90-135mm. It is known as the Yellow-necked mouse due to the yellow-brown patch or streak on the underside of the neck and on the chest between the front legs. It is browner than the Wood mouse.

The Wood mouse (*Apodemus sylvaticus*) is smaller, with a head and body length of 80-105mm and a tail of 70-95mm. However, as measurements are taken on adult animals, juveniles of the two species may be confused.

The diet for both species is very similar to that of the fancy mouse, although they do enjoy the addition of animal protein (for example, high protein flaked fish food or insects, such as mealworms, once a week).

Naturally, when organizing housing for these species, their highly active behavior must be taken into account. Ideally a cage for these would be one with a nest area that could be isolated from the remainder of the cage. This would facilitate cleaning and avoid the danger of individuals escaping. A converted aquarium is probably best. Litter material would be either a peat or forest bark shavings or sawdust mix. Both of these would prevent odor and the need for frequent cleaning and would also appear more natural to both the animals and owners. I would suggest that the nesting material be of hay or a combination of hay and paper bedding. Hay should be included, as small amounts of it are eaten by both these species. Nestboxes will be used, if provided, as well as branches and twigs for climbing on and chewing, and exercise wheels. Small amounts of food will be stored by both these species and these or at least a smallish part, should be left in the storage area when cleaning out, unless, of course, it has mold on it. Water bottles should be available at all times. Generally speaking, both species are retainable in groups or pairs, although overcrowding should be avoided. A population ratio of approximately four to six individuals in an area

36x18x12 inches is recommended. Breeding and gestation are similar to that of the fancy mouse.

THE DEER MOUSE

The Deer mouse is also known as the White-footed mouse. This is really the name of one particular group and depending on which reference books you consult, you will find between 16 and 60 different species and sub-species of this group of mice listed. All are known as *Peromyscus* and all are found in North America, from Alaska and Canada south to Mexico and Central America. All may be treated the same in captivity. In size they vary from 70 to 170mm, with a tail length of an additional 40 to 205mm. Naturally, the coloration also varies greatly from sandy gray to chocolate brown. The feet and underparts are usually white, although just to confuse matters, some individuals have been known to have dark gray underparts and black feet.

As with all mice, if you decide to house them in an aquarium or any type of cage, please be careful that the wire is of a suitable diameter.

Other Species of Mice

These more wild species are prone to escape by squeezing through the wire and are also quite capable of jumping three feet from a standing start. Plenty of twigs and climbing areas should be provided; equally important for this species are hiding places. Litter should be in the form of large flaked wood shavings, forest bark, peat or a combination of all three. Again, by using the combination, cleaning is cut down. Cleaning out as frequently as once a week for this species will disrupt the animals and may cause fighting. They also store a great amount of food and disturbing this store will also lead to "unnatural" behavior. Plenty of hay or dried grass—not straw—should be provided for nesting material.

Deer mice will often take some time to settle down once moved to a new cage or home and thus may be slow breeders. It is also known that some brother/sister matings often fail to produce litters at all and that interbreeding is not tolerated for more than five generations. Some believe that lack of protein in the diet leads to infertile pairs. This may be helped by providing the addition of flaked fish food or insects to the normal rich seed diet. These species are much more capable of eating a rich diet than the fancy mouse and are thus more suited to the foods sold for hamsters and gerbils.

Introducing strange individuals may be difficult, as the species can be very territorial and defend their cages against other members of their species. Thus, pairs are safest, with young being removed at approximately 30 days of age. Allowing for their jumping abilities, deer mice are not particularly difficult to handle and do not often bite.

HARVEST MOUSE

The Harvest mouse, *Micromys minutus*, is one of the smallest of all the rodent species, measuring only some 57mm in length. In appearance, it is perhaps not so mouse-like as its name implies. The face is blunt, its eyes do not bulge, but are small and black and the ears are small and relatively inconspicuous, projecting only slightly out of the russet colored fur.

It is, however, an easy species to keep and breed in

captivity. However, having said this, it is not all that widely available.

Being so small, the harvest mouse requires a special type of cage with very narrow bars. Generally I would suggest that a tall cage be provided for successful breeding. For the best effect, this should be tall enough to contain a good amount of tall grasses.

The bottom of the cage should be provided with a fairly deep litter of peat or forest bark. Soft meadow hay should be provided for nesting and should a good amount of grasses be provided, you will find that a nest will be built in the tall grass using both the grasses and the hay. If you provide extra twigs and sticks, it will encourage the building of

A female spiny mouse.

a nest above the ground.

A female Harvest mouse in captivity, in a suitable cage, may produce nine to ten litters between the age of three and eighteen months, with an average of 3-4 per litter; they may live for up to five years but rarely breed after 18 months. As the young mice mature at about 4-5 weeks of age, they may be attacked by their parents and so should be removed to a separate cage and paired up either in single or mixed sexed groups.

(Although the above is about the European species, American Harvest mice may be treated the same.)

NATAL MULTIMAMMATE MOUSE

Although a number of sub-species and species occur in this group of mice that most commonly seen in captivity is *Mastomys natalensis*, the Natal Multimammate mouse. (It should be noted that this mouse is also known by the scientific name *Rattus natalensis*.) In appearance it is rather more rat-like than mouse-like. The fur is soft, dark grayish above, with grayish white belly. It is 15-25cms long, with a tail of about 11cms.

The species was first introduced to captive breeding in 1939. It is surprising that it is not more widely available, as it is widely retained in laboratories, especially in South Africa. Over the years, like the Mongolian gerbil, the species has become quite docile and certain colors have appeared, although I do not believe these are available outside South Africa at present.

The name multimammate is derived from the unusual number of teats that the female has—up to 16 pairs—which lie on the belly and the chest. Even so, the average litter rarely exceeds eight. The young are born after a gestation period of 21-26 days. At birth, they are covered with sparse hair and are independent at about 27-30 days.

It is an easy species to cage, not being particularly inclined to chew the cage itself. However, they do require a rather large area in which to mate successfully. For this, a pair appears to have to be able to chase about the cage when the female is in heat. It seems that without this chasing the female will not conceive and produce a healthy litter so easily, although this is not always the case. A cage should be about 90cms long and tall enough to allow a number of branches to be included for climbing and running about on. A nestbox of some form should be provided, with an additional storage area.

Generally, towards other rodents, the Multimammate appears non-aggressive; to its own species, however, it can be cannibalistic. This ranges from the normal eating of the afterbirth to the entire litter, dead or ill cage mates, and, on rare occasions, healthy cage mates and even themselves. This is generally only associated with very inbred stock and a good sign to look out for are chewed and nibbled tails.

As with a lot of rodents, litter-eating of the first litter by females does occur and this may be excused. A female that eats her first litter will often go ahead and raise a very good second litter. Females in overcrowded conditions or those with little chance to hide both themselves and their young are the most prone to

eating their young. Retaining in pairs and the removal of young at weaning, as well as the introduction of dark nest boxes, should all help.

I have never found this species difficult to handle or sex.

Diet is also easy. They will eat just about any type of seed, grain, cereal, or nut. They will also take quite large amounts of vegetables, fruit, and grasses.

SPINY MICE

Spiny mice are immediately recognizable by the thick spiny hair growing on the back. They are found over most of the drier parts of Africa, as well as the Middle East and North Western India, and the islands of Crete and Cyprus. There are approximately seven species and 28 subspecies.

In Europe and the UK, three varieties are retained. The most commonly seen is the Arabian or Cairo Spiny (*Acomys cahirinus dimmidiatus*); the other is the Egyptian Spiny mouse (*Acomys cahirinus cahirinus*), and the last is the sub-species of the Golden Spiny mouse (*Acomys russatus lewisi*). Of these three, the Golden is the largest, while the Egyptian is the smallest, averaging about 4-5 inches between the three. With few exceptions, all can be regarded as the same species in their captive treatment.

Adult Arabian Spiny mice have a pale yellowish beige back, while the youngsters are a pale pearly gray. All ages have white underparts. The back and base of the tail are covered with coarse, rigid grooved spines. The tail, as with all spiny mice, is scaly and nearly naked and very brittle, rather like that of a lizard. For this reason, spiny mice should never be picked up by the tail like the fancy mouse.

Egyptian Spiny are a uniform ash gray—again with whitish underparts—although not as white as the Arabian. The young are the same color as the adults.

The Lewisi subspecies of the Golden Spiny mouse is, in fact, a uniform black, or dark gray. The spines on the Golden are more widespread than those of the other species, starting between the ears and extending further down the flanks.

Spiny mice are social creatures and live most happily in colonies, although the Golden prefers smaller colonies than the others. Care must be taken, however, not to allow the colonies to get too big—with *any* of the species. Overcrowded tail nibbling can often result, perhaps through boredom as much as anything else. It may also occur on rare occasions when there is too high a proportion of males in a colony.

Being highly social creatures, nests are shared and several individuals literally pile on top of each other. "Nest" is really the wrong word to use, as with the exception of the Golden, spiny mice do not actually build a nest, but simply use a hollow in the litter or shelter under rocks or in nestboxes provided.

For such a small rodent, the gestation period is relatively long, being approximately 45 days, with an average litter size of just two. Unlike similar-sized rodents, the young are born well developed with their eyes open, furred, and able to run about the cage within a day or so. The female does not retire from her fellows when about to give birth and tends to do so in a standing position. Any female will feed any baby,

A spiny mouse. There are a number of species of spiny mice, all of which are distinguished by the spiny hair that grows on their backs.

and it is not unusual to see a female with a newborn feeding from one nipple and have an almost weaned baby feeding from another.

Babies are weaned at 14-21 days and become sexually mature at about seven to eight weeks of age, but their growth is not complete until they are about six months of age and even then they continue to put on weight. The average lifespan is 36-48 months.

As they are highly social creatures, I always suggest that spiny mice be housed in large glass aquaria (90x30x45cms). One aquarium could easily house 6-10 individuals. Be forewarned however: on the whole, the spiny mouse is a very talented escapologist. A tight-fitting lid is necessary, as the spiny is a very good jumper from a standing start. The aquaria should be furnished with wood shavings, sawdust or sand litter. They rarely dig, so this need not be very deep. Rocks, pipes, or even bird nest boxes should be provided to give the group place(s) to sleep and rest. Branches will be appreciated for both climbing on and chewing. A wire wheel will be used a great deal; a plastic one will probably last a short time, as the mice tend to chew these although, strangely enough, they rarely chew their cages.

Diet should consist mainly of various types of nuts, seeds, cereals, and biscuits. A small amount of meat, fish, or insects should be given once or twice a week. The meat may be in the form of scraps, such as leftover chicken bones. Vegetable food can be given, but unless you are sure that your animals are used to it, please only start them with small amounts. I have found that my animals are fond of avocados, pears, grapes, dates, figs, and bean shoots.

Spiny mice drink a remarkable amount of water and should, therefore, always have plenty available (from a water bottle).

Spiny mice are not easy to handle because of their spines, but they can (particularly the Golden) become very friendly to their owners. Some will come to the hand to take tidbits of food and some even answer to their names.

INDEX

Fancy Mice
KW-224